D1088672

Nick Hunter

Chicago, Illinois

www.capstonepub.com
Visit our website to find out more information about Heinemann-Raintree books.

To order:
☎ Phone 800-747-4992
⌨ Visit www.capstonepub.com
to browse our catalog and order online.

Edited by Rebecca Rissman, Dan Nunn, and
    Catherine Veitch
Designed by Cynthia Della-Rovere
Leveling by Jeanne Clidas
Picture research by Elizabeth Alexander
Production by Victoria Fitzgerald
Originated by Capstone Global Library
Printed and bound in China by CTPS

16 15 14 13 12
10 9 8 7 6 5 4 3 2 1

Library of Congress Cataloging-in-Publication Data
Hunter, Nick.
  Space / Nick Hunter.—1st ed.
    p. cm.—(Explorer tales)
  Includes bibliographical references and index.
  ISBN 978-1-4109-4782-6 (hb)—ISBN 978-1-4109-4789-5 (pb) 1. Outer space—Exploration—Juvenile literature. 2. Astronomy—Juvenile literature. I. Title.
  TL793.H796 2012
  530—dc23   2011041471

Acknowledgments
We would like to thank the following for permission to reproduce photographs: Alamy pp. 9 (© Peter Horree), 11 (© RIA Novosti), 13 (© ITAR-TASS Photo Agency), 17 (© AF archive), 27 (© Pictorial Press Ltd); Corbis p. 24 (© Stocktrek Images); Getty Images pp. 8 (NASA), 10 (Keystone/Hulton Archive), 12 (Bates Littlehales/National Geographic), 14 (SSPL), 15 (Time Life Pictures/NASA); NASA pp. 7, 16, 19 (Sandra Joseph and Kevin O'Connell), 18, 20, 21, 22 (JPL-Caltech), 23 (JPL-Caltech), 25; Science Photo Library p. 26 (Steve Gschmeissner); Shutterstock pp. 4 (© Nikm), 5 (© Sebastian Kaulitzki), 6 (© Anteromite).

Cover photographs of an astronaut reproduced with permission of Shutterstock (© eddtoro); Northern and Southern Celestial hemisphere, 1880, reproduced with permission of Sanders of Oxford, rare prints & maps (www.sandersofoxford.com); Saturn reproduced with permission of NASA (JPL). Background design features of the solar system reproduced with permission of Shutterstock (© Anteromite).

Every effort has been made to contact copyright holders of material reproduced in this book. Any omissions will be rectified in subsequent printings if notice is given to the publisher.

Disclaimer
All the Internet addresses (URLs) given in this book were valid at the time of going to press. However, due to the dynamic nature of the Internet, some addresses may have changed, or sites may have changed or ceased to exist since publication. While the author and publisher regret any inconvenience this may cause readers, no responsibility for any such changes can be accepted by either the author or the publisher.

Contents

Some words are shown in bold, **like this**. You can find out what they mean by looking in the glossary.

Journey to the Stars

For thousands of years, people looked at the night sky and told stories about the **stars**. Since 1961, space explorers, or astronauts, have risked their lives to discover what lies beyond Earth.

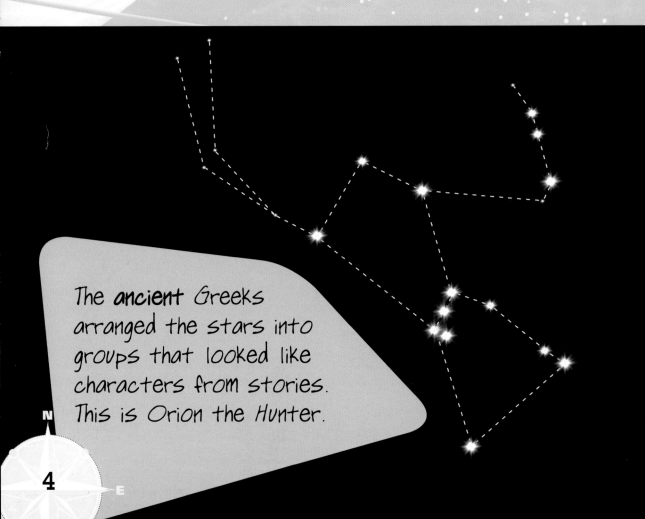

The **ancient** Greeks arranged the stars into groups that looked like characters from stories. This is Orion the Hunter.

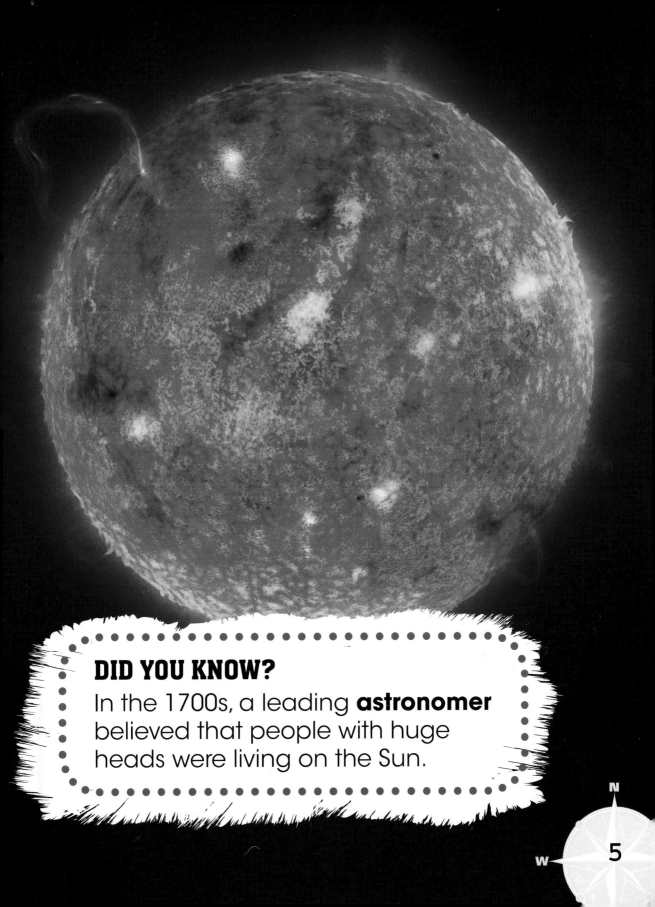

DID YOU KNOW?

In the 1700s, a leading **astronomer** believed that people with huge heads were living on the Sun.

What Is Space?

Space is closer than you think. Earth is surrounded by a layer of **gases**. Beyond this layer is space. In space, we can see the Moon, the **planets** of our **solar system**, and some of the billions of **stars**.

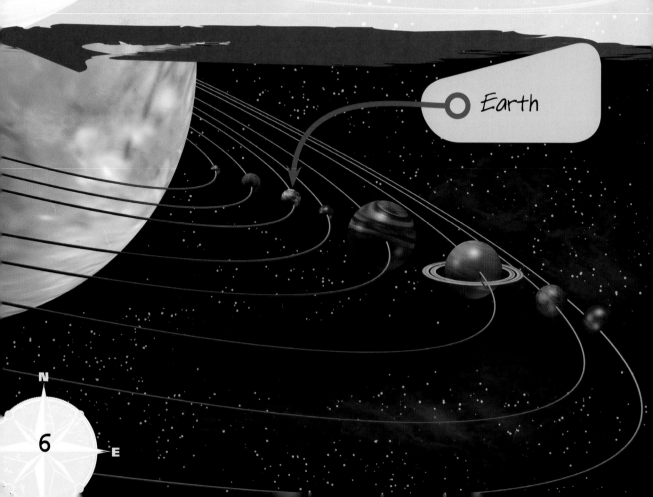

Earth

space junk

DID YOU KNOW?
Objects left behind by astronauts in space—for example, rocket parts—are known as space junk. A lot of space junk **orbits** Earth.

Into Space

After takeoff, spacecraft travel around nine times faster than a speeding bullet. Astronauts wear special suits to protect them in space. If you left a spacecraft without wearing a space suit, you would not survive for long.

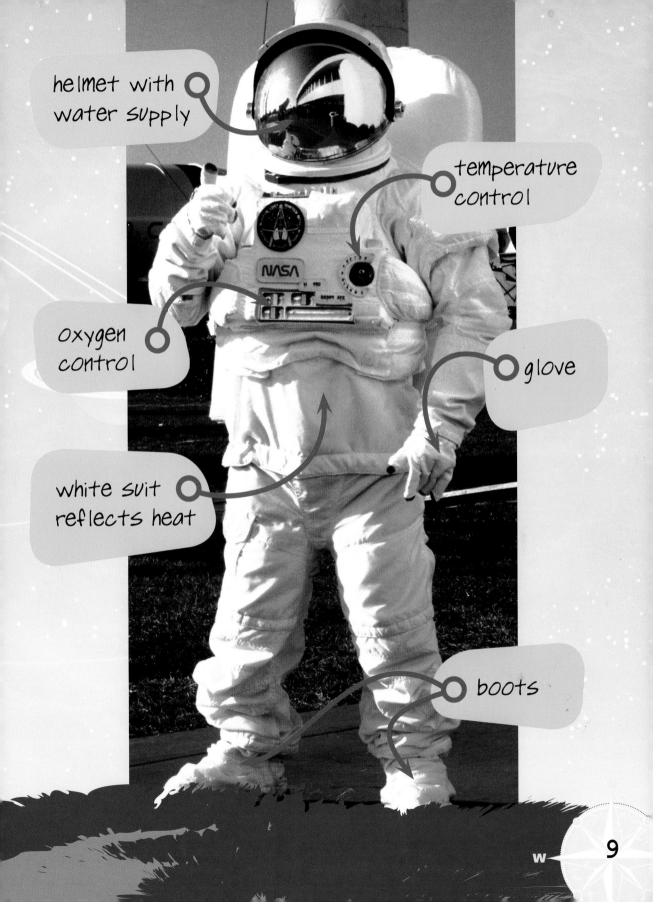

helmet with
water supply

temperature
control

oxygen
control

glove

white suit
reflects heat

boots

First Person in Space

On April 12, 1961, Russian astronaut Yuri Gagarin blasted into space. Gagarin was the first human space explorer. His spaceflight lasted only 108 minutes. It nearly ended in disaster when two sections of Gagarin's spacecraft failed to separate correctly.

Laika was the first dog sent into space.

DID YOU KNOW?
Several animals were sent into space before Gagarin, including a dog and two monkeys.

How Do You Land a Rocket?

Spacecraft are traveling at thousands of miles per hour when they start to re-enter Earth's **atmosphere**. The first U.S. spacecrafts used **parachutes** to slow down before landing in the sea.

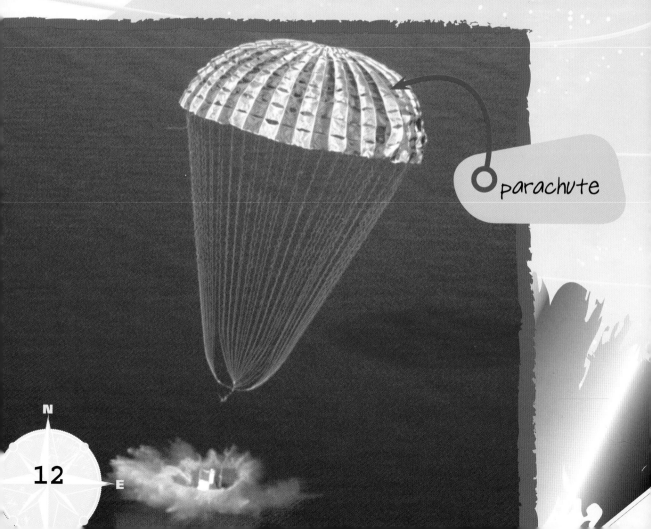

parachute

In 1963, Valentina Tereshkova was the first woman in space. Before becoming an astronaut, her hobby was parachuting.

Man on the Moon

On July 16, 1969, the *Apollo 11* spacecraft lifted off on its way to the Moon. The astronauts traveled nearly 240,000 miles to reach the Moon.

Michael Collins trains for his flight on *Apollo 11*.

DID YOU KNOW?
A modern cell phone has a more powerful computer than the spacecraft that took astronauts to the Moon!

Apollo 11

"The Eagle Has Landed"

Those were Neil Armstrong's words as *Apollo 11* landed on the Moon. Armstrong and "Buzz" Aldrin became the first humans to step foot on another world. Michael Collins remained on *Apollo 11* as it **orbited** the Moon.

Buzz Aldrin

A movie starring Tom Hanks was made about the *Apollo 13* mission.

DID YOU KNOW?

Only 12 astronauts have ever set foot on the Moon. *Apollo 13* failed to get there after an explosion.

17

The Space Shuttle

The space shuttle was launched in 1981. Blasting off while attached to the shuttle's fuel tanks was like being attached to a huge bomb. The rocket boosters could not be stopped until the fuel ran out.

drag chute

fuel tank

rocket booster

DID YOU KNOW?
The space shuttle was the first spacecraft that could be used more than once.

Living in Space

Space shuttle missions carried parts to build an International Space Station. Astronauts on the space station are doing experiments to help future space explorers.

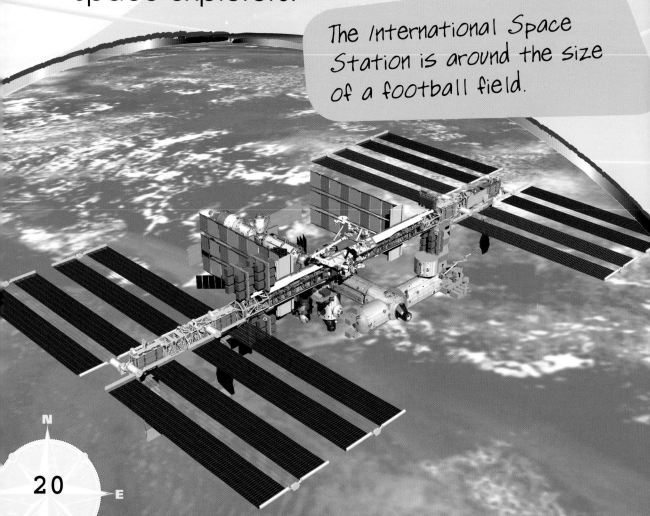

The International Space Station is around the size of a football field.

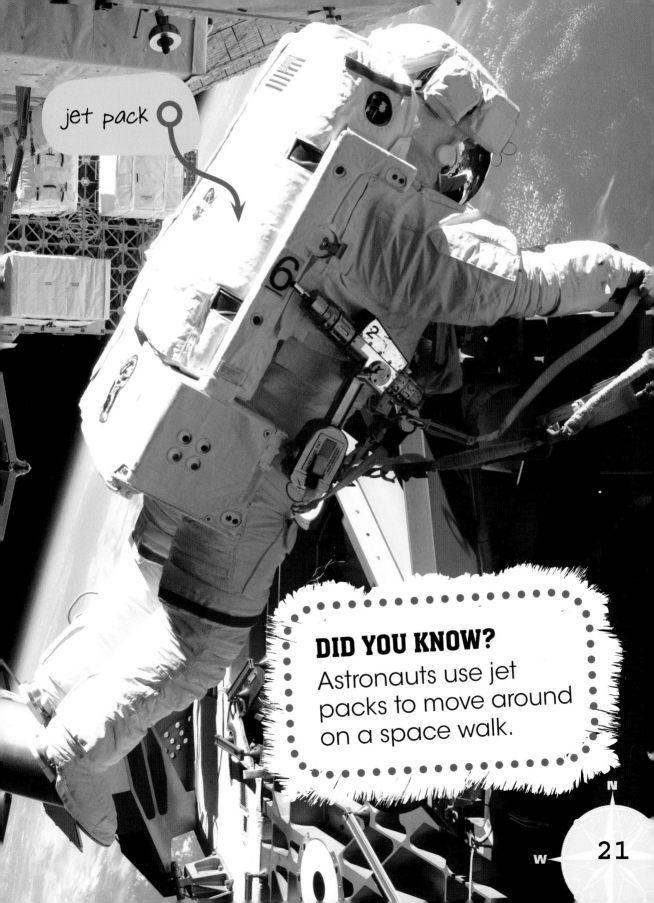

jet pack

DID YOU KNOW?
Astronauts use jet packs to move around on a space walk.

Exploring the Solar System

Humans have only explored the parts of space closest to Earth. The *Voyager* spacecraft have traveled to the end of our **solar system**, but not with astronauts on board.

Unmanned space rovers have explored the surface of the **planet** Mars.

DID YOU KNOW?

Mars is home to the biggest volcano in the solar system.

Mission to Mars

The **planet** Mars is the next target for space explorers. It would take at least a year to travel to Mars and back.

Long periods of **weightlessness** in space can damage the human body's bones and muscles. Exercising in space is important to help stop the damage.

Life on Other Planets?

Space explorers have not found life anywhere else in space. If there is life in our **solar system**, it is likely to be simple life like **bacteria**.

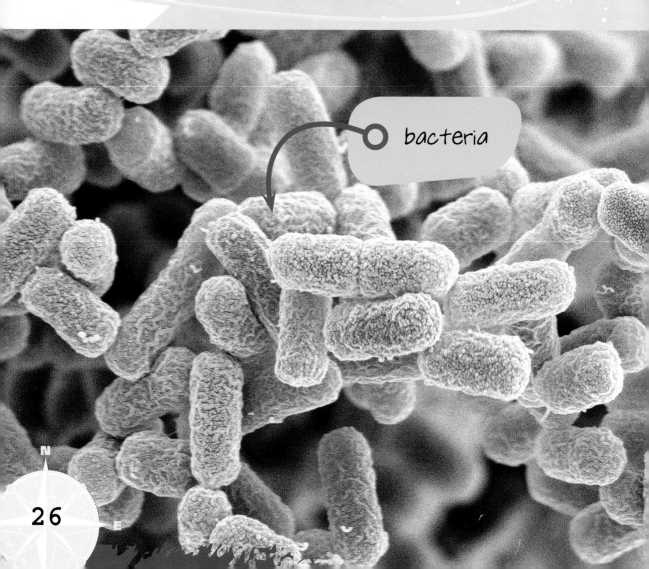

bacteria

There are billions of **planets** in space. Do you think one of them could be home to alien beings like the ones we see in movies and on TV?

Timeline

1957   October 4: *Sputnik 1* is the first craft in space.

November 3: Laika the dog is the first living passenger on a spacecraft.

1961   April 12: Yuri Gagarin becomes the world's first astronaut.

1963   June 16: Valentina Tereshkova becomes the first woman in space.

1969   July 20: Neil Armstrong is the first person to walk on the Moon.

April 17: The *Apollo 13* mission returns safely to Earth after an explosion during its mission to the Moon.

1981   April 12: The first space shuttle launches from the Kennedy Space Center in Florida.

Becoming an Astronaut

Thousands of people apply every year to become astronauts. Only a lucky few are selected. To become an astronaut you need to:

- O study hard at math or science

- O be physically fit

- O be an experienced military pilot

- O be brave enough to journey into the unknown

Do you have what it takes?

Glossary

ancient lived or existed a long time ago

astronomer someone who studies space

atmosphere layer of gases that surrounds Earth

bacteria tiny living things that can only be seen with a microscope

gas substance, such as air, that has no fixed shape

orbit path along which something moves around a planet or other body in space

parachute large piece of fabric that slows someone down when falling from an aircraft

planet large ball of rock or gas that orbits a star, the way our planet Earth goes around the Sun

solar system collection of planets and other bodies that go around the Sun

star huge ball of burning gas that produces massive amounts of heat and light

weightlessness when someone floats in the air, as astronauts do in space

Find Out More

Books

Fradin, Dennis B. *The First Lunar Landing*. New York: Marshall Cavendish Benchmark, 2010.

Gilpin, Daniel. *Spacecraft* (Machines Close-Up). New York: Marshall Cavendish Benchmark, 2011.

Tagliaferro, Linda. *Who Walks in Space?: Working in Space* (Wild Work). Chicago: Raintree, 2011.

Websites

school.discoveryeducation.com/ schooladventures/spacestation/
Find out more about the amazing International Space Station.

www.kidsastronomy.com/index.htm
Learn lots of facts about the solar system at this website.

www.nasa.gov/audience/forkids/kidsclub/ flash/index.html
Find games, videos, and lots of information from NASA, the organization in charge of U.S. space exploration.

Index

T 567776